CHESHIRE LIBRARIES	
PETERS	19-Nov-2008
£10.99	

EARTH

AND

MARS

Rosalind Mist

QED Publishing

Words in **bold** can be found in the glossary on page 22.

Copyright © QED Publishing 2008

First published in the UK in 2008 by
QED Publishing
A Quarto Group Company
226 City Road
London EC1V 2TT

www.qed-publishing.co.uk

All rights reserved. No part of this publication may be reproduced, stored in a retrieval system, or t ransmitted in any form or by any means, electronic, mechanical, photocopying, recording or otherwise, without the prior permission of the publisher, nor be otherwise circulated in any form of binding or cover other than that in which it is published and without a similar condition being imposed on the subsequent purchaser.

A catalogue record for this book is available from the British Library.

ISBN 978 1 84538 963 5

Printed and bound in China

Author Rosalind Mist
Consultant Terry Jennings
Editor Amanda Askew
Designer Melissa Alaverdy
Picture Researcher Maria Joannou
Illustrator Richard Burgess

Publisher Steve Evans
Creative Director Zeta Davies

Picture credits
(fc=front cover, t=top, b=bottom, l=left, r=right)

Corbis Denis Scott 14, NASA 2–3, 17b, 18–19, Reuters 18b

ESA 15t, 18t, 24

NASA fc, 1b, NASA Goddard Space Flight Center 1t, 5t, 7t, 15c, 15b, 21c, Goddard Space Flight Center 6, 23, JPL 16l, JPL/Cornell University 20–21, 21t, 21b, JPL/Malin Space Science Systems 19, JPL/USGS 16r, JPL-Caltech/University of Arizona/Cornell/Ohio State University 17t

Photolibrary Alaskastock 11b

Shutterstock 4l, 4–5, 7b, 8–9, 10–11, 12b, 13t, 13b

EDUCATION LIBRARY SERVICE

Browning Way
Woodford Park Industrial Estate
Winsford
Cheshire CW7 2JN

Phone: 01606 592551/557126
Fax: 01606 861412

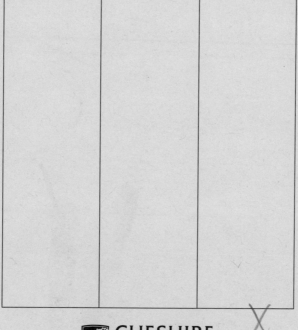

CHESHIRE
COUNTY COUNCIL

Contents

The Solar System

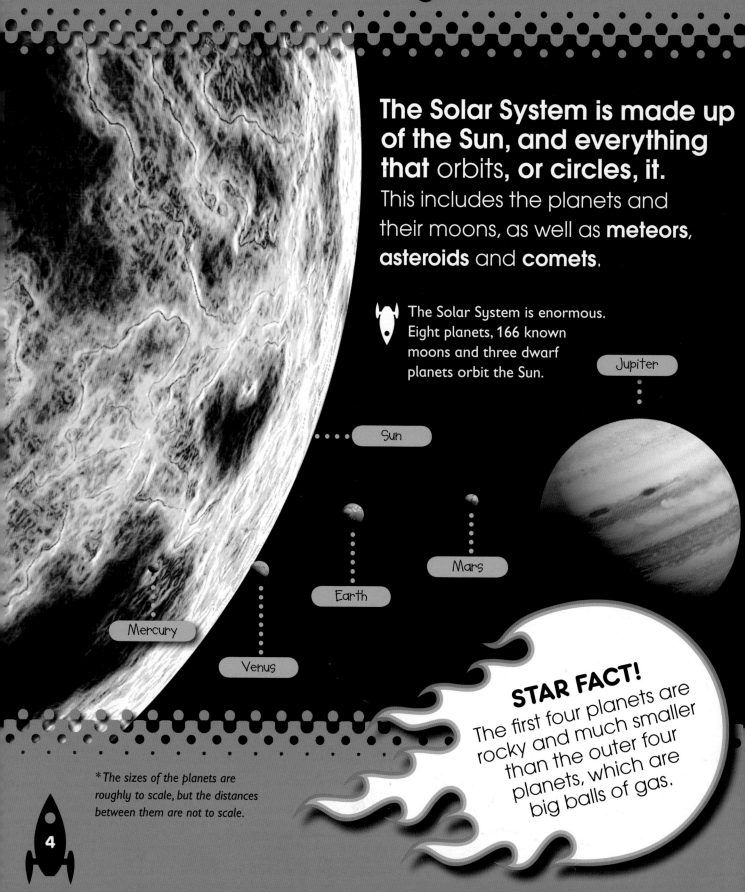

The Solar System is made up of the Sun, and everything that orbits, **or circles, it.** This includes the planets and their moons, as well as **meteors, asteroids** and **comets**.

The Solar System is enormous. Eight planets, 166 known moons and three dwarf planets orbit the Sun.

Jupiter

Sun

Mars

Earth

Mercury

Venus

STAR FACT!
The first four planets are rocky and much smaller than the outer four planets, which are big balls of gas.

The sizes of the planets are roughly to scale, but the distances between them are not to scale.

4

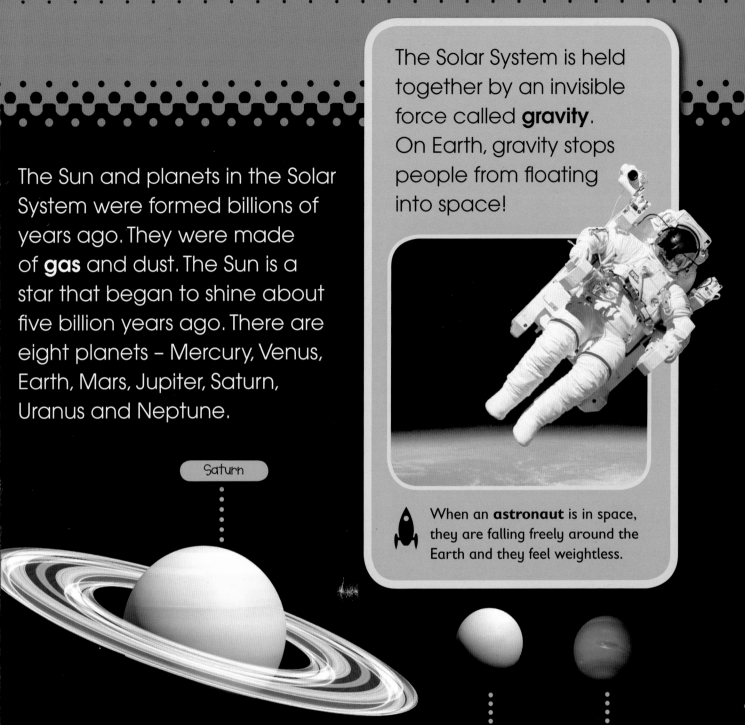

The Sun and planets in the Solar System were formed billions of years ago. They were made of **gas** and dust. The Sun is a star that began to shine about five billion years ago. There are eight planets – Mercury, Venus, Earth, Mars, Jupiter, Saturn, Uranus and Neptune.

The Solar System is held together by an invisible force called **gravity**. On Earth, gravity stops people from floating into space!

When an **astronaut** is in space, they are falling freely around the Earth and they feel weightless.

Saturn

Uranus

Neptune

Planet Earth

Earth is the planet we live on.

It is the third planet from the Sun, between Mars and Venus. From space, it looks like a blue, green and white marble. This is because it is covered with oceans, land and clouds. In fact, 70 percent of the Earth's surface is covered by water!

STAR FACT!
The Earth formed about 4600 million years ago. It started as huge clouds of swirling gas and dust.

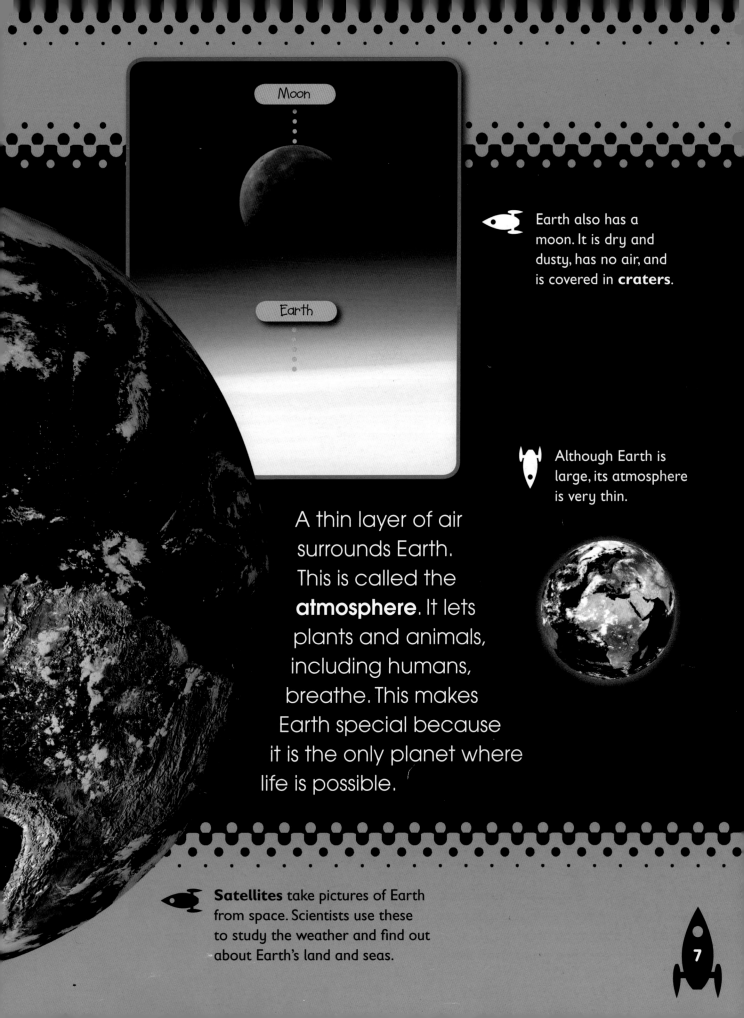

Moon

Earth

Earth also has a moon. It is dry and dusty, has no air, and is covered in **craters**.

Although Earth is large, its atmosphere is very thin.

A thin layer of air surrounds Earth. This is called the **atmosphere**. It lets plants and animals, including humans, breathe. This makes Earth special because it is the only planet where life is possible.

Satellites take pictures of Earth from space. Scientists use these to study the weather and find out about Earth's land and seas.

Inside the Earth

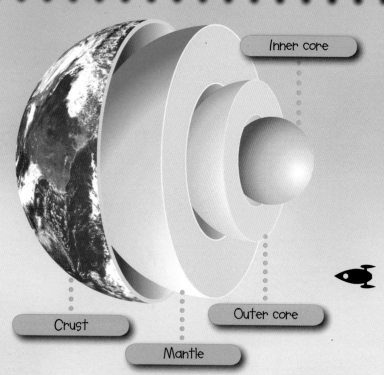

Inner core

Outer core

Crust

Mantle

The Earth is made up of four different layers.

The crust is the layer that we live on. It is made of giant slabs of solid rock that float on hot, soft rock underneath.

The Earth is like an onion, with four layers. To find out about the layers, scientists measure how earthquakes travel through the Earth.

Below the crust is a layer of hot rock called the mantle. In places, the rock is so hot that it has melted. This molten rock is called **magma**. When a **volcano** erupts, the magma bursts out. Then it is called **lava**.

STAR FACT!

Where pieces of crust bump into each other, mountains are pushed up, volcanoes erupt and earthquakes take place.

Next is a layer mainly of liquid iron called the outer core. The liquid iron swirls around and makes the Earth work like a giant bar **magnet**. The north pole is in the Arctic and the south pole is in the Antarctic.

The middle of the Earth is made mainly of solid iron. This is the hottest part and is called the inner core.

Eggy Earth

A hard-boiled egg is like the Earth.
Yolk – inner and outer core
White – mantle
Shell – crust
Ask an adult to help you to break open a hard-boiled egg to see all the different layers.

The magma, or molten rock, inside the Earth is very hot and soft. It can flow out of volcanoes in red-hot rivers of lava.

Day and night

The Earth spins around like a spinning top.
It turns all the way round in 24 hours – a day. In a day, the whole world, apart from the poles, will have daytime and night-time. Only one side of the Earth faces the Sun at any one time. Sunlight shines on this side and it is daytime. On the side that is not facing the Sun, it is night-time.

Daytime in South America

As the Earth spins, the Sun shines on one half of the Earth, and it is daytime.

Night-time in South America

When the same side turns away from the Sun, it goes dark and daytime turns into night-time.

Shadows

Stand outside on a sunny day and look at the ground. Can you see your shadow? Or try making different shadows using a torch and a piece of paper – it will work best in a dark room.

At sunset and sunrise, the sky can turn red and orange or even pink.

WARNING!

Never look straight at the Sun. It is so bright that it can damage your eyes.

When the Sun seems to go down, or sets, your part of the Earth is turning away from it. This time of day is called dusk. When the Sun seems to come up, or rises, the part of the Earth that you are on is turning towards it. This is called dawn.

In summer, in the northern part of the world, near the Arctic, the Sun never sets completely. It is light for 24 hours a day. This is called the midnight Sun.

During the day, the Sun rises and falls, making a path across the sky.

The seasons

The Earth orbits, or circles, the Sun.
It takes a year to go round the Sun once.
In this year, we have four seasons – spring,
summer, autumn and winter.

The Earth's **axis** is tilted. As the Earth moves
around the Sun over a year, the amount
of sunlight in different parts changes.
When northern areas, such as Europe
and America, are tilted towards
the Sun, it is summer, but
when they are tilted
away, it is winter.

The seasons occur
because the Earth's
axis is tilted. When
one part of the Earth
points towards the Sun,
it is summer. When the
same part points away,
it is winter.

STAR FACT!
Seasons in Australia are the opposite of those in Europe. When Europe is tilted towards the Sun, Australia is tilted away, and vice versa!

Summer

 In summer, the days are long and the
Sun is high in the sky. The weather is
warm and flowers are fully grown.

In spring, the Sun gets higher in the sky and the days become longer. Plants start to grow and baby animals are born.

Spring

In winter, the Sun is low and the days are short. The weather is cold and many plants die.

Winter

In autumn, the days begin to shorten and the Sun is lower. It is cooler and trees lose their leaves.

Autumn

Mars, the red planet

Mars is the fourth planet from the Sun, between Earth and Jupiter.
It is about half the size of Earth. The planet is red-orange in colour because it has rusty-red soil.

Mars

Earth

Mars is covered in hills, craters and volcanoes. The planet has no liquid water. There are no seas or lakes.

Mars has a dry, rocky surface. Scientists think that Mars used to have liquid water, but now the only water that has been found is in the polar **ice caps**.

 The surface of Mars looks like a dry, rocky desert. The Mars Exploration Rovers have to find their way around the rocks as they explore Mars.

Phobos

Deimos

 Phobos and Deimos look like asteroids. They may have come from the Asteroid Belt.

Mars has two moons called Phobos and Deimos. They are chunks of rock, much smaller than the Moon. They are covered in craters. Phobos speeds around Mars once every 7.5 hours. Deimos takes 30 hours to orbit, or circle, Mars.

STAR FACT!
Sometimes Mars has a pink sunset because of the red dust in the air.

On Mars

Mars has a volcano called Olympus Mons – the largest and highest volcano in the Solar System. It is about three times as tall as Mount Everest, the tallest mountain on Earth.

STAR FACT!
Olympus Mons covers almost the same area as the British Isles.

Victoria crater

Olympus Mons

Valles Marineris

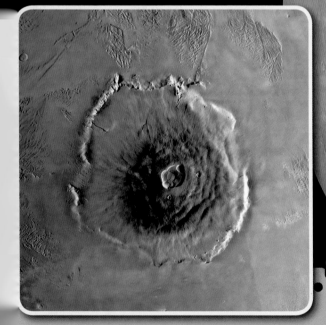

🚀 Olympus Mons has not erupted for at least two million years.

Make your own craters

Fill a deep bowl halfway with sand, salt or clay. Drop different stones or marbles into the bowl. Look at the shapes of your craters.

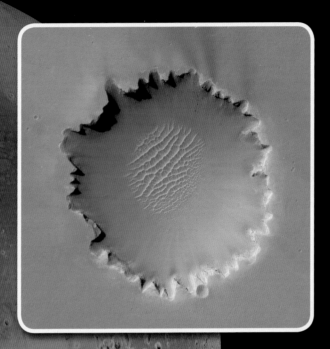

 The Victoria crater is about 750 metres across. The Mars Exploration Rover, *Opportunity*, is exploring it.

When a large rock crashes onto a planet or moon, it leaves a big crater. Mars is covered in lots of craters.

Valles Marineris is the biggest canyon in the Solar System. It goes nearly a quarter of the way around Mars!

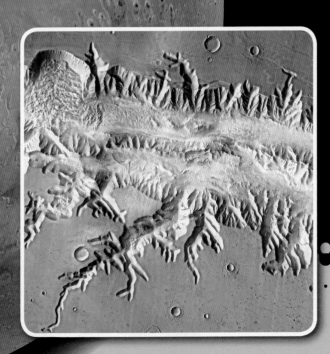

 Valles Marineris is enormous, at more than 3000 kilometres in length. The Grand Canyon in the United States would fit into just a small part of it!

Stormy planet

On Mars, there can be very fast winds.
Sometimes the whole planet is one big dust storm!

STAR FACT!
On Mars, there is very little water, but sometimes there are thin clouds. It never rains on Mars.

 The red areas are dust from volcanoes and the dark areas are rock. The dust is blown around by the wind in huge dust storms.

Mars has dust devils, which are swirls of wind and dust – like mini tornadoes. The robotic rovers that are exploring Mars get very dusty. Every time the swirling winds of a dust devil go by, the rovers get cleaned.

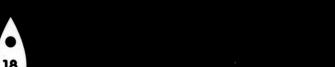 Dust devils on Mars can be small and gentle, but they can be much bigger than those on Earth.

A long, deep valley near Mars' north pole. The light and dark areas show layers of ice and sand.

Christiaan Huygens (1629–1695)

Christiaan Huygens was the first person to see a white spot on Mars. We now know that this is an ice cap. Huygens also found out that a day on Mars is nearly as long as a day on Earth.

Ice cap

Mars has ice caps, just like Earth. By watching the ice caps on Mars, scientists worked out that Mars has seasons, too. In summer, the ice melts and the ice caps get smaller. In winter, the ice caps grow again.

Exploring Mars

Lots of space probes **have visited Mars.** Some have even landed on the surface.

In 2004, two Mars Exploration Rovers, *Spirit* and *Opportunity*, landed on Mars. They are like large remote-controlled cars. Scientists on Earth drive them slowly over the planet. They have climbed hills and explored craters.

Camera

Antenna to send information back to Earth

Tool to collect rocks

 Spirit moves slowly to make sure it does not get stuck or miss anything interesting.

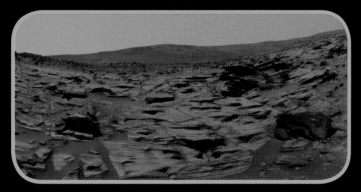

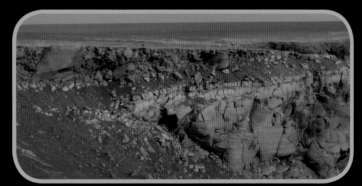

By looking at what types of rock there are on Mars, scientists can work out what Mars used to be like.

The rovers can take photos of Mars. They can also measure how hot it is there. They have special tools to test the different rocks and can even collect dust from the air.

The rovers have made many discoveries. Scientists now think that there may have been liquid water on Mars a long time ago.

STAR FACT!
The Mars Exploration Rovers were only meant to work for three months, but they are still working after more than four years.

Glossary

Antenna
A wire that is used for receiving radio and television signals.

Asteroid
A large lump of rock, too small to be a planet or dwarf planet.

Astronaut
A person who travels in space.

Atmosphere
A layer of gases around a planet or moon.

Axis
The straight line through the middle of a planet or moon that it spins around.

Comet
An object in space made of rock and ice.

Crater
A hole made on the surface of a planet or moon by an asteroid or comet.

Gas
A substance, such as air, that is not solid or liquid. Gas cannot usually be seen.

Gravity
Attractive pulling force between any massive objects.

Ice cap
Layer of ice at the north or south pole of a planet or moon.

Lava
Molten, or liquid, rock that has cooled and turned into a solid.

Magma
Hot, runny rock from the middle of a planet or moon.

Magnet
A piece of metal that can attract iron or steel. It points north and south when held in the air.

Meteor
A glowing trail in the sky left by a small piece of rock from space.

Orbit
The path of one body around another, such as a planet around the Sun.

Satellite
A man-made object that orbits the Earth.

Space probe
A spacecraft without people on board.

Volcano
A place where magma comes to the surface.

Index

Light travels in straight lines. Shadows are a good way to show this. If light could bend around corners, there would not be any shadows.

Try using a ball and torch to simulate day and night. Mark a spot on the ball, and then shine a light on it. As you spin the ball, the spot moves in and out of the light.

Where have the craters gone? The Earth and the Moon are the same age, but the Moon is covered in craters. Earth has had craters, too, except that most have now been destroyed or hidden. The tectonic plates that make up Earth's surface continually move. This, and the associated volcanism, has destroyed some craters. Wind and water erode the surface, too. Soils and the seas hide others.

Why is Olympus Mons so big? The volcano was made by lava flowing out from under the surface of Mars. The lava stopped flowing a long time ago. This would not happen on Earth, as the top layer of the Earth's surface is moving all the time. As the surface layer moves, it moves the volcano away from the hot spot underneath and a new volcano forms. This is why there are chains of volcanoes on Earth. On Mars, there are no plates so the volcano stayed in one place and grew ever larger.